Shoes of the Wind

A Book of Poems

By Hilda Conkling

Published by Pantianos Classics

ISBN-13: 978-1986229227

First published in 1922

Contents

To a Mother

To a mother with hazel eyes and brownish hair,
And fingers quick as stars
That twinkle in night-cold air...
Hair wound like a web of lacy sea-weed...
Blue robes floating like the spring wind...
My mother has a heart that loves me
And sings like a music.

Locust Tree in Bloom

A bough of locust blossoms for my present,
Or just a spray is enough for me!
They smell like honeysuckle and poppies
Twined together ...
Their buds hang like green fruit...
They are shoes of the wind.

Poems

I know how poems come;
Thy have wings.
When you are not thinking of it
I suddenly say
"Mother, a poem!"
Somehow I hear it
Rustling.

Poems come like boats
With sails for wings;
Crossing the sky swiftly
They slip under tall bridges of cloud.

Lilacs

After lilacs come out
The air loves to flow about them
The way water in wood-streams
Flows and loves and wanders.
I think the wind has a sadness
Lifting other leaves, other sprays...
I think the wind is a little selfish
About lilacs when they flower.

Through the Rainbow

Through the rainbow I saw blue hills.
Songs love that country.

Spring Talk

Two cherry trees are showing white
And the plum tree is in bloom.
Apple blossoms are opening...
Come to the crab-apple tree!
Come see the red buds peeping out!
When I shut my eyes
I see violet plants drawn on my eyelids

From picking violets all day long;
And there were just as many
After I went away
For every violet I picked
Two more sprang up...put on their purple or
white...
When I did not see them
As quietly as Bumble-Bee
Decorates himself with pollen
Whenever I'm not looking.
You'd better look at my last-year's garden!
All my golden-glow is flourishing,
My trillium has a big huge bud...
It is warbler-time, blossom-time,
Past pussy-willow-time, time for willow leaves,
With ferns uncurling, bloodroot petals scattered,
Wild honeysuckle turning red
Among the rocks...

June Day

I've had a good time today, Mother!
I feel happy as a starling on a cherry-bough.
Young plants coming...
Apples swelling...
{But the biggest of the feelings I know

Will always be cherries ripening in the light!)
The song of the catbird touched my heart.
I swang in the breeze with my thoughts floating around me…
Thoughts of little robins
Trying to eat cherries,
Thoughts of baby grackles in their nests
At sunset-time,
These were in the shade, these were soft-colored thoughts
Under the apple-tree as I swang…

Marigold

Marigold, marigold,
Where are you going?
Have you a plan? Can you not tell me?
I should like to know!
There are lots of places to wander,
There is a brook needing a visitor,
A robin needing a friend.
You must not be lonely:
You belong to nature as I do!
You have a frank little way of staring…
I am curious about you!
The blue sky hangs over you and me…

The sun's rays fall on us both...
Why not be happy
On this wonderful earth?
Marigold, answer!
I tell you all my thoughts
But you have not said a word!
(I was then she said softly
"I have many friends.
But you are my best!"

Drowsy Island

I know where a crested island
Bows his head to a wave that is full of stars...
Lays his cheek against the foam of that wave.
It is where the sea is dark
Against the edge of the world.
It is farther than ships go.
When I am sleepy
I see trees move all shadowy...
Strange fan-curved shapes moving slowly...
There are no trees like those
In this valley!
It is so far away,
Surely I do not hear them rustling,
But what is the sound in my mind?

Waves can make it, murmuring up a beach...
Leaves can whisper that way
At night...

Edge of Morning

Gray slate roof of a house near by
Turned silvery by the sun...
Clouds keeping their grayish night-pink...
Then suddenly
Sunlight poured through the windows;
Sunlight sang as it came;
Clouds dashed by singing;
The blue sky coming opened its eyes to the sun.
This is a picture-poem
But it is my thoughts, too!

Golden Wave

The golden wave of sunset
Stays long...does not flow away...
Red-rose color and pearl
Above the amber twilight,
Gleaming like dew
On the leaves of the forest:
As though a great pitcher

Were pouring out light
I see the golden wave
Cover the world.

"I Won't Tell You the Name of This One!"

Softly, softly,
Gently, gently,
Over the tree-tops to the sky,
Back again to the hills,
Footsteps lost, footsteps unseen.
Always vanishing...

Softly, softly.
Gently, gently.
Don't you make a noise now!
This wonder-creature comes
But once a year...
Comes on tiptoe
Looking under leaves...
Softy, softly.
Gently, gently...

(Was it the wind?)

Dying River

The river waits for water
From a feeding stream;
The little stream, winding,
Runs on its way to pour itself
Into the dying river,
And the river lives again
In the valley.

Dreaming of Dreams

Dreaming of dreams long ago
On a rain-cloudy day,
I felt your soft hands like roses,
And your eyes looking down on me.
Your lips were near
Curled at the corners like flower-petals.
I think of your dark yellow hair
Lifted by the wind...
I can see it in my mind:
It makes me wonder.
How did I find you in my dreams?
Where is the dream now?

Where?

Your dream is flying over mountains
Down the valleys,
Over the rivers of autumn colors
Into the sky
And away!

The Key to My Mind

A little stone door in my mind
Opens and shuts with a musical sound.
There is a gold key
Locks the door;
The door is carved like lace.
Spirits fly in and out,
Messages
Of love and things I ought to know.
Through the lace-work of stone
Comes a sweet melody saying
Happiness...purity...strangeness...

Exiled Primroses

Two exiled primroses
Stood by a breaking wave.
Their mother was calling,
They could not hear.

They used to live beside a pine tree
In the garden of a rich merchant
Of a Chinese city
That had a name like music of gongs
Struck softly after dark.

Western Horizon

On the sands of the western sea
Are pink shells...bits of coral...
One lonesome shell
Holds my mind upon it.
Where the horizon bends
Ships pass:
I am that little shell
Watching them turn and go.
I hear waves break and fall away...
They are echoes in my heart.
They are stories I heard
Yesterday...
Often I try to remember to tell you
The words of their loveliness.

Moss

Green velvet to look upon,

Shaped and woven of tiny trees,
Soft velvet to make a pillow for birds
Or flowers when they go to sleep,
Velvet rugs for the footsteps of the wind
(Though he leaves no footprints behind him,)
I too have felt that softness:
I have heard the wind pass and return
And stoop down to whisper
Among the trees of the moss-forest.

Arbutus-ing

You hunt here and there,
You know not where,
And pull away the moss;
You think you won't find any...
But then!
A clump of pink and white ... all wonderful!
Now you think they are gone,
Now you almost step on the flowers
They are so near!
Small, clustered, a sweet breath...
Not a perfume,
Only a dark deep sweetness
Of arbutus....

Cloudy Pansy

Wandering down a dusty road
I met a gypsy.
She might have dropped out of the trees.
She had a green kerchief
And a blue velvet skirt,
A lavender cape
And a gold locket:
Green shoes on the feet
That trod the powdery road
To the marble-floored Vermont river
Thinking ... as it goes along...

Orchid Lady

Tan and green orchid,
Are you a little lady
Holding up your skirts
Above wet grass?
Do you wear a feather
Where that white is showing?
Is there any color
Shut inside your heart?
I could be an orchid,
I could be a lady,

I could wear a feather,
I could step like you;
There is just the difference
Of your way of bowing,
And your tilted bonnet
And your satin shoe!

Poppy's Sleepy Shell

Pollen of poppies ... a powder the fairies use
Out of the poppy shell of golden royal blue,
When they are going to dance and dance
In ring-abouts of mushrooms at night
Till poppies put them to sleep at last
With bedtime chimes and secret breath!

Rose Thistle

A Brook to run past it,
A cloud to float over it,
An eagle with its children
To talk to it,
The thistle on the hillside
Is pink with dew
And rainbow cloud.
Two bees dig out honey as hard as they can

Before the shower:
The humming bird eats honey too,
And later he will want thistle-down for his nest
When the rose-color has gone
And the flower is changed.

Autumn Blue Mist

This is night's own trailing wind
That goes by in blue mist
When morning wakes.
This is not smoke from chimneys,
No fire breathes and puffs it out
Across the sun.
This is autumn on an October morning...
Early hills,
Fields in a veil.

Moon in October

The moon is at her crystal window
Spinning and weaving...
The moon looks out of her window of crystal.
She has no lights excepting stars
That hang on threads unknown
From her sky-ceiling, her walls.

Their twinkling is like the twittering of many
birds
In the early morning.
The moon sits by her crystal window;
She sings to herself and spins...
Spins the pale blue silken thread
That holds earth dangling
Over deep light....

{Now this is what the moon sings:)

Spin, spinning wheel,
Day and night too!
I keep it going all the time
To weave my robe of dew.
I make it from the fields of blue
And the robin's breast;
The sun gives me rays
From the yellow west.
It shall be touched with evening
And with mellowy dew,
And send a separate shining
Down the sky to you,
My woven gown of sun-rays,
My silken gown of blue.

Nine

Do you know how nine comes?
The fairies have numbers, all my ages,
Sharp on a piece of card-board:
They cut out and spirit out my number,
Nine...
They come to the window softly...
Then they give it life...open the window.
It flies in, it bumps me on the forehead.
But does not wake me:
Just before morning breaks it fades back into my
brain
And is my age.

Wishes

I WANT three things;
They are wishes
Bright and happy.
You cannot know my dreams,
The wishes that stay in my heart...
I want three things
Unknown to any one!

Tell me — oh, tell me

What are the wishes
In your heart?

I cannot tell you;
It is a secret thing.

Mary Cobweb

She was not exactly a doll...
I always saw her taller,
And she liked flowery dresses
And gloves of violet petals.
Yet she was cozy and heartsome,
She could cook mushrooms
And knew how to season a roast.
Quite practical!
I called her Mary Cobweb
Because I knew one day that must be her name,
Though nobody told me:
And the secret fairy ways she had
Kept me interested in spite of my growing...
(Though now I have lost her!)
I know she liked cream...
I know she could not leave a honeycomb
Unbroken...
Somehow she was real

Through my own feelings....

To A Black Pansy

Little Prince,
Why do you stray about
Like a firefly who has lost his lantern?
Why do you sob,
Small gypsy in the dark?
Do you think maybe the world
Will end tonight?

Bare Butter-Nut Tree

A tree stands old and worn;
The North has blown away its leaves.
When I see it that way
I wish Spring would return...
How can I wait so long?

O butter-nut tree,
Why didn't God give you speech,
And you without your green leaves?
Why can't you sing small songs
Against the wind
For comfort?

Leaves

IN my apple-orchard
In the oldest tree
Fall has hidden gold leaves.
I looked into the hollow
And saw no apples,
Only leaves with frost on them
Like marble tilings,
Like jeweled tables...
Yet there was no gold ... no marble...
Only leaves covered with frost
That sparkled the way my thought told me.

My Mind and I

We are friends,
My mind and I,
Yet sometimes we cannot
understand each other;
As though a cloud had gone over the sun,
Or the pool all blind with trees
Had forgotten the sky.

River

Something wanders among the mountains,
Something ripples along forget-me-not fields,
Something cries when birds go south,
Something curves its golden sand-bar
Like the handle of a purple sword.
If I speak strangely
Do not wonder:
Something is looking for a castle
Made of seaweed, shells and coral,
Where the sea curls
Under the sunrise.

Evening River

There's a cloud in the west
Shuts the big red globe from my eyes.
Two little clouds
Are sundown birds sailing past in pink light:
Stars on dwindling threads hang trembling:
Birds come and have soft talkings together...
Company sometimes, maybe?
But now I am leaving in blank thought that river
Murmuring its poem about the sun,
About the sand and glittering stones...

Oh pure white sand!
Now I turn away to strange moments
And places...
Now the evening curls and doses....

Wet Day

Rain-drops slanted down,
Light struck through them sharply...
The sun burst through...
It was like a thunder cloud
But golden.
Everybody was shut into houses
On this favorite street of mine:
Even I had been shut in.
But when I saw the rain-drops parted,
I stood free:
The sun-god swept his wind over us.
He flung glory into our feeling of clear relief...
People of the town
Tired of rain.

Old People Singing

I love to listen to old people singing.

I love the way they have of humming to them-
selves.
It makes me think of the sun of past days
That is the present...when it shines again...
It makes me think of lonely trees
Strayed away from their forest...
It is like a thick soft curtain hiding the view from
me
Of a country I have never seen.

Japanese Picture

Trees on a marble island,
Birds with little brown backs...
Is this Paradise?
Mountain of my heart
With pink and purple coloring,
Little houses on the river-bank...
Houses made of maple-sugar,
Distant tree,
Boats with blue sails;
Japanese people in silk
Hidden in the brown-sugar houses;
Yellow sky, pearl-colored ground,
River-ripples like the ripples in silk
Or a windy corn-field;

Hills of pink opal
And dewy seas...
Did you answer my question
About Paradise?

This Is A Dream

Roses in my garden,
Brooks that run far,
Clouds that go a-hunting,
Red copper fountain-bowls...
This is all my dream
I am telling you...
Candlesticks, palaces,
Leaves that turn to gold,
Marble shapes that stand,
Trees that turn to silver,
Leaves of glass,
(Roses in my garden,
Brooks that run far...)
Oh my dreams will be coming true
Some day when I do not think of it!
Love is my dream,
Love is everywhere.
(Brooks that run far
Reject the sky.)

Love climbs like a vine
In my heart;
Like a vine of amethyst
And pearl.
Oh, my dream will come true some day,
Roses in my garden, brooks that run far!

Wood Dove

When morn in breaking
When the sun is rising over dark blue hills,
When mists go by
I hear a voice say
Coo...coo...
It is Mistress Wood Dove
Hidden and alone,
Glad of morning,
I call,
She answers:
Morning is sweeter
For her voice.

Jasmine in Spring's Hair

Jasmine in Spring's hair, braided into Spring's hair,

Dangling stars wound closely,
Stars fluttering from the braided golden wind,
Spring mist melting out through trees
Over peacock-fern....

All the time mist lifting...
Mist going away...going away...

Jasmine like a Spring moon
Growing on the blue vine of night...
Jasmine shining in the hair of Spring
And the scent of jasmine coming into my
thoughts....

AH the time the mist lifting slowly...
All the time the thought of Spring on tiptoe in my
heart....

Message for A Sick Friend

Tell her my love
Tell her to go to sleep
Thinking of everything in the world;
Colors ... the wind...
Or a fish in a spray of opal seaweed...

August Afternoon

Sea-Blue of gentian,
Blackberries' ebony stain,
Yellow of goldenrod,
Tree fringes wavering along the road
Under the hill,
These make up an August afternoon
I have known:
But more than fruit or flower or tree
Is my mother's love I hold In my heart

Chrysanthemums

Dusky red chrysanthemums out of Japan,
With silver-backed petals like armor,
Tell me what you think sometimes?
You have fiery pink in you too...
You all mean lovelmess:
You say a word
Of joy.
You come from gardens unknown
Where the sun rises...
You bow your heads to merry little breezes
That run by like fairies of happiness;
You love the wind and woody vines

That outline the forest...
You love brooks and clouds...
Your thoughts are better than my thoughts
When the moon is getting high!

Bluebell Ring

Bluebells all in one
Like a piece of sky,
Nodding to the faint air
With still faces,
Stirring a little,
Holding their breath for wonder
But all the time friendly
To any one who passes....

Nature

Sitting in the half-dusk,
My mother and I talking and gossiping...
(Such gossip! Such talk!)
We tell poems,
We wonder over nature, what she can be about?
It would be strange to ask questions of nature
And *be* nature at the same time!
Nobody knows what secrets she has

Hidden in her bosom white like a shell.
My mother does not know, I don't know,
Nobody knows.

Gold Fish

Like a shot of gold
Or an arrow darting
With thin gold wings
He swims...
Now around...then straight...
Then a swish of tail...
Then zigzag all along
With a kind of stiff smile...
In ponds or bowls
He swims and stares
Out of big popping eyes
Of ebony...

Barberry

I'm going to have a horse
Named Barberry,
His coat the color of barberry leaves
In autumn:
Russet red he will be

With flying mane,
Strong and wiry,
His head slender and haughty!
Touch him...feel the life and joy within him
Run through you like fire!
He will be free as wind:
He will take me through forests away from peo-
ple,
Fast lakes, across rivers, into the mountains:
He will go galloping across corn fields by twilight
He will find me a coral beach.
His eyes will snap with joy of always being free.
People may give me their best horses...
Barberry for me, against them all!

Joy

JOY is not a thing you can see.
It is what you feel when you watch waves break-
ing,
Or when you peer through a net of woven violet
stems
In Spring grass.
It is not sunlight, not moonlight,
But a separate shining.
Joy lives behind people's eyes.

Field Mouse

Little brown field mouse
Hiding when the plough goes by,
Timid creature that you are,
Wild thing,
Were you once in the forest?
Did you move to the fields?
In your brown cloak
You gather grain
For your secret meals:
You will build a house of earth
The way you remember:
From a baby up to your fullgrown feeling
You have run about the field
As other field-mice will run about
When another century has come
Like a cloud....

Moccasin Flower

"Moccasin flower," I said,
"Like a ship full of thoughts
Floating down a river,
Thoughts I don't know In the little ship's heart...
Moccasin flower of the woods,

Wild May orchid,
Looking out at the weather
And the moon's rays,
Who is it you play with?
Daisy or buttercup?
It cannot be,
For you live in the forest,
They, in the fields.
Do the robins come to visit you,
Or bluebirds, maybe?
Do they bring you cherries
For your gown?
I wonder if you know them.
They are friends of mine.
Do you know Mrs. Primrose?
She wears a pink gown...
You must be friends!"
A small voice answered
"I know her very well,
But not Robin, Bluebird,
Buttercup or Daisy!
I know Fern, Red-Cap Moss, Mushroom,
I know Wild Canary, Hermit Thrush,
Brown Veery comes at sunset...
I have often seen him...

I have heard his thoughts
In tones like apple-blossoms,
The kind a violin plays...."

Suddenly I noticed dusk
Coming...
I heard the veery...
I tiptoed away.

Butterfly Adventure

I saw a butterfly
Dark-brown and dusty
Like a plain traveler.
But when the sun shone on him
He wore sapphire-blue and opal
And winking half-moons of gold powder...
All the brown vanished away!

How could I know
He was iridescent?
Nature seems to hide
When you look at her with sleepy eyes,
But with eyes wide-open in the open light
You see her shine to all the colors
Of the sun.

Carrier Pigeons

Across the rippled ocean
Where the wind blows wildly
And never keeps still,
Across the midnight sky, a glad news!
Messages floating, beating,
Happy words high over the sad sand
And empty waters...
Pigeons on their way
Home.

Cherry Blossoms

Artificial, lying on the bough like snow-flakes,
With pinkness touching them sometimes
As though it were sunset,
Cool and far-looking
Yet turning all the time into red ruby cherries...
I am waiting with the robin redbreast
For the hour to come!
They will be green, then daffodil yellow,
Then their cheeks will redden,
They will be ruby-dark that now are hidden...
The far will change into near....

I am watching you every Maytime hour
You artificial rosebud-snowflake cherry blossoms!

The Cellar

I love my queer cellar with its dusty smell,
Its misty smell like smoke-fringes
From clouds blowing past;
With its shelves of jam and goodies,
With its boxes...barrels...
Woodpiles here and there.
There is a passageway
To an unknown room
Where bins hold carrots and things.
There are glass doors that bang
And cobweb windows.
I love the quietness of my cellar
Thinking in the dark.
My cellar has apples in its breath,
Potatoes even,
That smell of earth.

Peony

Shell-pink it stands in the tall glass,
Queen Elizabeth in a ruff (or one of her ladies?)

Looking the way she did in old English times.
To see her makes me hear fiddlers playing
Out-of-doors!
I can never tell which they will be when they
come out...
King or queen or lady of the court...
Country woman or man or little laughing girl
Dancing through the woods...
Very soon that peony over there
Is going to be Cinderella;
But this is Queen Elizabeth
In my mother's vase.

The Milky Way

Down the highroad of the Milky Way
We go riding
On horses made of stars.
The clouds flit like white butterflies;
We are dry ... we do not know it is raining
Upon earth.
Roses of opal and pearl
Sway back and forth in the musical wind...
Pine trees like emeralds hang...
A pheasant's wing like a fan is spread...
White mountain-peaks gleam...

Purple and silver is the sunrise.
Quiet lakes shine along the Milky Way
Like mirrors you hang on cottage walls.
When I am asleep
This is what I shall dream.
Things can never really go,
They come again and stay
 When your thoughts are put on beautiful things
They come alive and stay alive In your mind.

Geranium People

Clouds were flying up out of the water.
Hills were like blue asters against white surf.
The wind blew from nowhere, from everywhere.
It did not know where it was going.
I saw red geraniums like falling stars,
Their heads still upright, though sunflowers were
drooping;
When frost comes,
And the bleating hail,
These geranium people will not be strong
Any more.

Daisies

Snow-White shawls...
Golden faces...
Countryside, hillside, wayside people...
Little market-women
Selling dew and yellow flour
To make bread
For some city of elves...

The Old Brass Pot

The old brass pot in the corner
Shines and scowls at the kitchen pans;
Like a stubborn king
He sits and frowns...
Orders them about
When I'm not looking.
He was a gift from the fairy queen...
What can I do?

He boils rice when I want it,
Makes broth when it is needed,
He is magic
But he growls all day.

Without him it would be pleasant and comforta-
ble
In my little cottage
With wistaria growing over the open windows...
What can I do?
He tells the frying pan
To stay on its hook...
He shouts at the other pans
In a gruff voice...
They all might be so happy
In my cozy kitchen I
Tell me...but you must whisper .
What can I do?

Night Is Forgotten

Night is forgotten.
Birds sing when the happy sun
Looks suddenly down.
I hope the iris is out
With dew like jewels fringing the petals;
I hope the oriole is up
Arranging his feathers.
I must hurry...there is so much to see...
I can hardly remember it all!
Only yesterday I made a song about a yellowbird

And what did I say?
It is not real to me now
Though I know how he gleamed,
Shining through four thin leaves
Of the pear-tree.

Elsa

My sister stood on a hilltop
Looking toward the sea.
The wind was in her bronze-colored hair.
She was an image
On a broken wave...
Foam was at her feet.
So for a moment she wavered
And was lovely;
And I remember her.

Hill Song

Away, away on a winding road,
Away, away, far and wide to the mountains,
Through pleasant meadow-plains that smell of
strawberries
Down a lane of mountain-rue
We go.

All this will fade away,
But here we are on the road to the hills
To the sky where swallows flit
And shove their wings into the mountain-air.
They slash their wings into the brook-water,
Let it flapper over their wings....

(In the fields, strawberries dark red with ripeness,
In the brook, trout that wear coral beads.)

It is the gurgling of brook-water
Makes me want to sing!
This hill-song is over now...
Ends suddenly
Like a sapphire....

Apple-Blossom Town

I know an orchard...
Apple-blossom Town!
Bees live in the next village.
Pink and fluffy houses in the trees
Are for rent.
My thoughts tell me who will come...
These are trees that blossom with bees and birds.

Here is a town with just enough air, just enough sun;
Love enough, happiness enough.

Bed Time

I look at the clock of the moon...
Time for children to be in bed!

I have hidden the great sleepy ocean
Under a leaf:
I have talked to the mountain softly
As I would to a thrush;
The river is stretched out
In the cornfield,
But there is still a commotion in the lower valley
Where I tethered the west wind to a sycamore
tree.

Pigeons Just Awake

As the sun rose
Everything was bathed in gold,
Trees were still and solemn...
Pigeons waded the dew.

Their feet were the color of new June strawber-
ries.
I thought what it must be to fly,
To whirl up into the light,
To know the curved flight of pigeons
Above trees and lawns!
If I could fly I should not have to leave my mother
for long
Nor my dark-eyed sister;
Only a fluttering, a lifting
Up round the elm tree and over,
A cool curving and sliding down the light
Into wet grass.

Little Old Woman

Bending down like arms
The branches of the crab-apple tree
Make a shining tent
With doors of glass I can look through
And green satiny doors
Each with a lock of gold.
I sit like a little old woman knitting
In the Spring warmth...
The spots of sunlight on the grass
Are golden children singing and dancing;

My arms are full of golden children,
Though I do not know what they sing ...
Little old woman that I am,
Knitting....

This Is About Mountains

It's maple sugar time
In the mountains.
The brook has climbed its bank
To look over into the world.
Trees are beginning to think...
They stretch themselves.
The bareness of the woods will go
If the pattern of the year is what I learned
Last Spring.

The mountains I knew best
Used to have festivals...
There was September on Starr King...
I remember the apple-sauce tree,
I remember how I would smash apples on top of
a rock
Crush them with a stone for the calves to eat.
How the chipmunks scolded me for taking the
apples!

Chipmunks own the mountains
But the mountains haven't heard about it yet.
March maple-sugar and September apples
And a cave of honey the bees know,
And Hilda to think about them
Afterward....

Horse-Chestnut Cottage

Within a green and everlasting covering
Like a coat of mail
There lives a little old lady
In an apartment of several rooms.
The walls are pink on one side,
Brown on the other;
She must be a rich old lady to have wall-
coverings
Of changeable silk finer than spiders' webs!
Once she got lost.
I saw her shiny shriveled face
Look up at me
From the grass.
I heard her call and call me
In a faint and shivering voice
To come to her quickly,
Unlock the door for her,

Help her up the steps
Into the place she had always known
Since she began at all...

Magnolia

Oh shell-pink that you wear,
Oh pure white bosom!
Like a fan all spread,
Like a sail ready to go over lapping seas,
Sometimes birds flutter in your branches,
But you have not many friends.
Your friends are flowers,
Your comrades are trees,
But birds seem shy of you.
And the little insects.
I know not what your thoughts may be
When the wind blows your flower-buds
Single or in clusters.
Oh beautiful magnolia
Up against the gray stern sky!
Your color lightens the grayness
And purples the rain.

Hermit Thrush

Something that cannot be said in words...
Somethmg sweet and unknown...
The wind ... the brook...
Something that comes to a trembling fuller tone
Like a waterfall...
That little brown creature is singing
A music of water, a music of worlds;
He will fly away south,
But his song stays in the heart
Once it is heard.

Flitting Wave

Three words I combine
Mix them like a wine
For the sea to drink:
Happy...merry...gleeful...
These are three words
That sparkle!
The wind sings with foam.
I, with my thoughts.

The Sea Is Gray

The sea is gray with a gold rim of moonlight:
Foam is the lace binding the golden rim.
Only a tittle while ago
The sea was an opal box.

I have buried my thoughts in the sand:
It would take a water-creature to find them.
I could not find them myself with much searching
Unless a shell should remember for me,
Or a sand-cricket mark a pebble-mound...
"Here you hid something!"

Once I cared for many things
I have forgotten.
When the sea moves slowly
Nothing matters except the moon.

Moth

By the river of Now-a-days
When you bend close to see the million tiny flow-
ers
That crowd to make one bloom of the Queen's
Lace,

If you happen to disturb ray secret dream,
I shall come flitting like a small moth
Into your mind.

Honey

There's a busy hum in the farm meadow
As the bees go from daisy to clover-top
Humming, bumming as the horizon clouds blow
nearer,
Humming, humming on this gay June morning.
Even the vineyards are in bloom:
The grape-flower breath comes on the breeze
Something like breath of primroses that bloom in
evening light
And laugh at what goes on in the world.

Dryad

Don't scold willows,
They are dryad trees!
If you find a dryad,
Dolores, my dear,
She will kiss you, maybe…
Make you young again!

Today I Saw

Today I saw the world a new way:
Close-drawn slanted rain, white light, the wind
blowing,
And the sky with a fringe of elm-buds.

Let the rain now fall in torrents
And the trees shake like flags:
Today I saw the world a new way.

Let the sand-dunes have their song.
The Connecticut swept by them proudly
Fluttering her silver skirts of rain
So that I thought of all the queens I have ever
known
In all the stories.

The Song

The pine tree was singing a song tonight
With the wind in its branches,
But earth-held children were heavy with sleep:
No one heard the song.

Wild Tulip

Mottled like the tiger-lily leaf,
With black necklace clinging,
(Of course it has a green cloak!)
 God has made a tulip.
He made the glacier like a moving jewel,
He made the tulip
Like a red cloud lighted by the sun.
I wonder how it feels to make a flower
Or a glacier like a great dream!

Lustre Cup

The rainy blue teacup is my favorite.
It has a mountain like a white butterfly
Poised...
It has a lake with coral reeds.
I see water-hyacinth growing,
And I know flamingoes
Will come flying over.
A strange voice tells me to go searching...
Tells me I could find something on that shore
No one else can find.

Volcano

In Mexico a mountain stands alone.
It looms above me ... a joy strikes my heart;
I see its transparent colors, its long opal hair...
But the moon would make it shine
A heap of silver.
My thoughts are gone from me
Because of that splendid trembling iridescent
thing...
I know it will fade,
I know it must go.
Songs float over its crest...
Dusk is coming on...
I will touch the mountain!
My fingers touch air.
The broad bright country sways in folds
Like long slow waves...
If all the hills were water rising and falling
This would be the highest wave,
This would be the white-hooded wave,
This would be the great wave for sea-gulls
to follow!

May Basket

Not violets, not lilac,
But cowslips to remind you of the marshes,
To tell you how the redwing is back
On pale-feathered willows;
Cowslips wading in water ... I found them wading
Up to their little green knees....

Sunbeams

Sunbeams sing little folk-songs
About fairies, about Neptune
And those old gods...
Sunbeams remember the world being made:
Grasses and small things
Remind them.
I have heard them speaking another language
As though the sun-god heard.
But I can understand better their oriole-talk
And their songs of delight
After rain.

Shadows

Circles transparent, black as night,

Circles with gold spokes of sun-rays,
Transparent as sun that shines,
Transparent as moon that beams,
Clear shadows whirl and flit.
As I think of it
Transparent is the whole spinning world.

Dragon Box

Carved and twisted and silver in its shadows
Is the dragon box my mother gave me:
Secret even from my sister
And friends dear to me.
I hide my treasure under the dragon
Curling on the cover.

Now it is a butterfly
On the blue velvet...
But sometimes it is my thoughts.
The butterfly is made of yellow opal.
With blade jet like two eyes
His wings are set,
And a dim black circle
Like a trail of strange thoughts.
I have told you about the butterfly...
I have not told you what I am thinking.

That is a dragon-box secret
Only Mother and I know.

Bulbs

Bulbs in brown capes
As though they were dead...
As though they would never come alive!

But their life is real
Though you cannot see it:
White ribbons reach from them far and wide
Into mysterious water:
When you have given up all hope...
(How can you know their narcissus thoughts?)
They soften and rouse
And poke out green finger-tips.

Three Hyacinths

Three hyacinths grow gaily
In the blue Chinese jar:
My mother, my sister and I!
We are curly-fingered,
We wear pointed caps:
We play ring-around-a-rosy all day long:

We look at winter through a silver window
Glad we are not made of frost,
For hyacinths on window-panes
Fade and vanish...
They cannot look back at the sun
Laughing softly;
They cannot whisper together, I suppose,
As garden hyacinths do,
Or as my mother, my sister and I whisper and
play
Living in the blue jar.

Snow Morning

Morning is a picture again
With snow-puffed branches
Out of the wind...
With the sky caught like a blue feather
In the butternut tree.
I cannot see the world behind the snow,
But when I look into my mind
There with all its people and colors
The world sits smiling
Quite warm and cozy.

Gold-Fish Bowl

Through the gold-fish bowl
I look into tropical islands.
The great bowl of water makes things bigger than
they are...
Stranger.
That is why one spray behind the glass
Keeps me dreaming of a palm tree;
And our reflected windows
Are a water-place.
The fish swim into one window...
Out of another...
Winding their gentle way
With no sound.
The bowl reflects and sings with color
And with my thoughts.
My mind whirrs and spins round
Thinking of things I'll see when I'm grown,
Thinking of what is in the world beyond
Waiting for me,
While I stare and stare into the gleamy bowl
Where gold and silver fish twinkle by
Weaving their web of shining trails. . . ,

Loveliness

Loveliness that dies when I forget
Comes alive when I remember.

A Memory

I picked up three folded tulip petals
That fell from a flower-head;
Pink and white they were, rolled a little
At the edges ...
When suddenly they smelled like pea-pods
Fresh and small,
And I remembered the Champlain garden...
How we shelled peas out-of-doors
And I ate the pods sometimes,
They were so sweet!
The whole tulip will not smell that way,
Only a few curly petals
Fallen,
If they are not withered and their own breath
Is about them.

Wreck

Sunfish like doves in the sea-trees...

And down below, a wreck
On the floor of sand.

That ship was a radiant ship
Sailing the going waters
To a sea far...far...
Those waves that dash against the rocks.
They are the same waters
That took the ship in their arms...

What I Said

Lilies of the valley,
Bell-shaped moments clustered,
Doves of time, little white doves
Through the dusky sunset-colored air
Set free,
I stroke your wings,
I stroke your folded wings.

Orion

I saw Orion glitter
Through the dark-boughed elm-tree;
And though I am little, though I could not know
or imagine

How he came there,
I knew how beautiful he was.

Blue Jay

All the flowers are sleeping,
A feather blanket of snow
Over them.
Blue Jay balances on a dry old sunflower's bent
head...
He dives under...
He strikes out seeds with angry beak.
His wings are barred with frost,
His snow-dusty feet
Are like dull crystal.
I like him...almost...
But must he keep on screeching in such a voice
And the flowers at their wits' end
For a little quiet?

April is Coming

APRIL is coming with wings of mist and scent of
lilac...
April is trailing her arbutus and-her ground pine
over hill-slopes...

April is making us new things to look at
Red-ruffled maples and pussy-willows turned
powdery,
You may see them through her transparent wind.

Ups and Downs

Mountains reach up skyward;
Boulders reach into the earth.
Mountains are great and strong, are royal when
you look at them:
Boulders have their minds on the center of the
earth
They came from.

Moonbeam

Moonbeam steps down the silken ladder
Woven by Mrs. Spider
To ask her to spin him a net
To catch the stars.

The Lake

The lake is solemn;
Its smiles are gone.
No swan, no birds

To get relief from burdens and dust.
Let me go make it glitter,
Make its flowers sing and blow
Into a little tune like a wind blowing
Or a poem Keats thought of...

Chinese Silk

Over the sea a wandership,
Over the sea a ship with sails of silk
Above the marble-white decks.
Silk with dragons of green,
Purple mountains,
Silk like a garden of colored gold and silver
With dolphins playing in a square pond;
Silk like a proud park
With a botd-plumaged peacock in a tree...
Rainbow and amethyst and gold.
I see fish with twinkling fins...
I see stars in water...
I see winter frost
Fringed with sunrise and sunset...
Maybe I see more than this
Tall sails full of pictures!
Silk from far-away China
With pictures coming alive

In the wind!

Song for Morning

Free to the wind like a swallow,
Free to the wind like a bird,
Over clouds, over fields flying always,
Never resting from the blue air,
Over brooks curled like ringlets,
Over apple-trees in flower,
hat is where I would be;
Free to the wind, free!

Weaving Laurel Dance

There's a path that leads
Through two squares of laurel
Where I dance like a nymph
In the April light.
I go through...out on the other side...
Back again...winding...
Twice again I weave my dance
And wander away among the trees.
I shall go back to dance again
When the laurel blossoms come,
When the May sun tinkles

Through the deep pines.
Stately the pines will wave over me
While I am in my weaving laurel dance....

Lilac Bush

Lilac princess
Swaying in a lavender gown,
She looks at no one
But straight into the eyes
Of sky and wind.
She may be sad when the rain comes,
She may be glad when it goes,
Always she has a smile
To give the world.
The sun beams on her,
Gives his glittering rays,
Helps her to remember
When she was in bud.
In clusters ... a lavender torch...
She trembles ... is alive...
Swaying in the lovely light
Of evening.

The Wave

Oh if I were a wave
With sea-green hair and white foam-dress,
Oh if I were a wave
With foam-white hair and sea-blue cloak,
I would go seeking oceans
No man has discovered,
I would go on...night or day the same searching...
Always singing to myself.
Somewhere golden sands,
Somewhere a beach of palms,
And the wind in them...
Ships to lift and swing like children...
Deep-sea things to handle
With my strong fingers of water,
Never a wish to be quiet
Very long...
Oh if I were a wave
With thoughts of seaweed
And dreams of sand and shells

Music

If I think music,
It comes and goes.

If the fountain ripples and splashes,
It keeps on singing.
Falling broken water
Sings and answers
When the warblers in the May trees
Stay close for a little.
But music that I hear
Is different in its meaning...
Happy hour or sorrowing
Into change.

Iris

Whiter than snow, sharp whiteness,
With fanning leaves, small and straight
Like herself,
With head to the sky
And violet eyes wide-open,
Iris comes murmuring a song
As trees do,
And leans upon the wind.
Later she droops her head,
For the dark
Has caught her...

Thoughts

Along a cloudy river
Comes the note of the evening dove
Like a mellowy light
That glimmers and is gone.
I shall remember my twinkling thoughts
That shine and are lost in the river.
Sitting on a mossy bank beside an oak tree
I see and hear and think...
All the great things of the world
Go by.
Even at six o'clock in the morning or earlier
There is the sunrise to think about.

When Moonlight Falls

When moonlight falls on the water
It is like fingers touching the chords of a harp
On a misty day.
When moonlight strikes the water
I cannot get it into my poem:
I only hear the tinkle of ripplings of light.
When I see the water's fingers and the moon's
rays
Intertwined,

I think of all the words I love to hear,
And try to find words white enough
For such shining....

Little Green Bermuda Poem

Green water of waves
On the Bermuda beaches:
White coral roads running away,
Pinks shells waiting for me to come:
I shall come some day!
How would it sound to be there alone
And hear the Atlantic Ocean
Crash on bright rocks?
This island is a great rainbow
That lasts forever.
People go and come
And the waves forget them.
I see the island turn and turn
A soap bubble with rainbows drifting down,
A rainbow ball turning...
Always light...always glitter looking through...
My poem that began with a green wave
Has broken into colors.

Thunder Mist

Whirling vapor changing....
Is it an opening flower?
Is it a fading prancing horse?
The steeple with its oldness,
In the foreground a maple with silver-backed
leaves
Against a violet cloud...
This is an August storm
That blew down out of the sky.

Brook

A rippling sound, a magical sound, a musical
sound
All in one,
The brook goes swirling, whirling.
Singing, dancing.
It likes to curl, and it curls:
It likes to whirl, and it whirls.
It comes to a long straight lane
And goes straight as arrows go.
Violets are the color of water
Under one kind of sky,
But water is always changing;

Going by.
This is a quaint song
You will not remember any more
After you have once heard it.
You cannot remember the sound of water
Nor the musical rippling of my words.

The Garden

Love is a garden
Where my soul is a tree In bloom,
Where my joy is a fountain that keeps rippling
Forevermore.

Hyacinth

Hyacinth, hyacinth,
Is it Spring now?
For I am weary of the long long winter
Green grass ought to come when Spring opens
her eyes,
Hyacinth, will you tell me
When Spring will be here?
The lilac-bushes are in bud
Under their snow.
I cannot see the buds

And no one tells me but you
Of the world coming alive
In the sun!

Butterfly in A Wind

All of a sudden
Blown to my hand
Wings of dewy color,
Silvery flaky dust along my finger...
I wondered where he had come from?
I asked him where he was going?

Butterfly words are faint
But I heard his answer...
I never know!
I am a wanderer in the wind.

I Keep Wondering

I saw a mountain
And he was like Wotan looking at himself in the
water.
I saw a cockatoo
And he was like sunset clouds.
Even leaves and little stones

Are different to my eyes sometimes.
I keep wondering through and through my heart
Where all the beautiful things in the world
Come from?
And while I wonder
They go on being beautiful.

About Animals

Animals are my friends and my kin and my play-
fellows;
They love me as I love them.
I have a feeling for them I cannot express...
It burns in my heart.
I make thoughts about them to keep in my mind.
I warm the cold, help the hurt, play with the frol-
icsome;
I laugh to see two puppies playing
And I wonder which is which!
General is a dog with blue-black eyes;
They shine...there is a love comes from them;
He is filled with joy when he guards me;
His eyes try to speak.
I see his mind through them
When he asks me to say things for him as well as
I can

Because he has no words.

Golden Pear Tree

Out beyond the hills
In a meadow there stands a pear tree
Like the sun.
It is a singing tree...
Its song is of the wind, of birds, of myself.
In winter time it is changed to a silver shape of
snow;
But before that time it has borne its pears
Of amber and gold.

Vermont Hills

The Vermont hills curve
Like a swirl of wind;
The last light shines...
They are like plums and grapes.
They have lights like coral,
Like April peach-trees in the dark.
I shall dream them again
When years have gone,
And I shall not have forgotten
You.

Eagle on The Mountain Crest

His bronze shone like a haze:
From below you would think him an image
Of long ago.
But he is real...he is of now-a-days:
No one made him but God.

I Wondered and Wondered

I wondered and wondered...
I saw a comrade of mine;
It was a wave smooth and blue
That tossed...fell away...
I wondered and wondered...
I saw a mountain white with old age;
I could not remember
How I came there.
I wandered and wondered
Under a motherly sky
That knew my name and kind,
That rested my tired thoughts,
That said *"I have a rainbow for you, Hilda,
And a young moon, hidden..."*

March Sunset

Pines cut dark on a bronze sky...
A juniper tree laughing to the harp of the wind...
Last year's oak leaves rustling...
And oh, the sky like a heart of fire
Burned down to those coals that have the color of
fruit...
Cherries...light red grapes...

Mermaid

Do not grieve,
Do not be unhappy,
Do not look about
As though you saw nothing!

Soon the black, the dark green ocean
Will come back...
Will clash against the rocks
On the sliding sand...

Soon the sun will come from the eastern horizon
Up from great blue hills
To change the water to glittering heaps
Of pearls....

Then you will remember!

Cozy Song

Cozy we sit
A cricket and I,
In a little tree-trunk corner
Soft with leaves of falling snow.
Friends are we.
For once he is not thinking
About music or moonlight.
We talk of a cottage somewhere
With a canary in the window
And chairs leaning together
Like old people talking;
It looks warm-hearted
To our dreams.

Dreams

Dreaming of lands far away
I lie on a smooth white cloud
Drifting along the wind
Lazy and slow-pouring above the trees.
They bend ... a quiet rush ... a hush...
A murmuring ... a rustle and swerve of leaves...
They are dreaming other dreams
Because they are old.

I do not know how it is
Dreams come to the old.
New worlds beginning when the old life ends.
Changing summers and autumns
With kind faces,
Spring-times that run away smiling...
Old people and old trees dreaming
Make we wonder.
There is not very much in my own dream today
Excepting thoughts that blossom in summer.
Whatever I tell you, O my mother,
You know I am only a little girl
Wondering....

Copper Bowl

When clouds sit in the sky
The earth must look to them like a copper bowl
With the sun on it.
I hope they see the green elm-buds floating in
that bowl,
And color like a lavender scarf
That is the April wind!

Pine Cone

Pine Cone is a brown girl
From Kentucky.
By a gleaming lake she stands
Like a lady in front of a mirror
Admiring her dress.
I often see her brown curls ruffled out...
I see her dimples...I hear the grass and the dew
play music to her...
But what made me think of her today
I'll never know.

Winter Night

The snow lies fluffed...
Untrampled.
The trees gossip when the moon gets up.
The music that is in the snow-dream
Stays with me,
Mother!

Song Nets

I weave them of sun and moonbeams;
I run back and forth making my nets.

The seagulls scream...
Tell me where to catch the songs;
I have a magic in my own mind
That tells me.

Song nets,
I weave you with all my love
You glitter like pearls and rubies...
In you I catch songs like butterflies.
You go past my reaching hand
With a thin gauzy floating...
And the songs are caught
Before they fade away.
Last night my hand caught a song
Of pines and quiet rivers:
I shall keep it forever.

I Live in a Cottage

There's a little cottage
in a ring of hedge.
Hyacinths grow
At the garden edge.
There's poplar and lilac
And an apple tree....
And there I am in my little red

dress and sunbonnet with the
watering pot in my hand...
Have you come to visit me?

Blue and Gold

BLUE of sapphire,
Gold of sunset,
In the lake they sometimes glitter,
In the sky they are often found.
Colors of sky and sun
Intertwined.
When the swans arrange their plumage
The blue and gold are like arms around them
Holding them close to the world.
Old as it may seem,
Tiresome as it gets to be to a young mind,
These two wonders, gold of the sun...
Blue of the sky and night...
Have to be thought about.

Royal Palms

There are thoughts in the earth
That grow to be palm trees.
Don't you hear the wind singing and moaning

Through their fanning leaves?

Bluebird

So happy the song he sings
On the apple-blossom bough!
Remembering how the sun
Melted the long winter snow.
He is the first to come,
He and his comrade robin,
In his heart joyful
Over returning Spring.
So happy the song he sings
On the apple-blossom bough!

Who?

Italian anemones in rose-mellowed purple
Are a window of color.
Who is looking through?

Trees

The clouds kiss the leafy breasts
Of the trees.
They tell me tales...they talk to me.
I will listen attentively to the tales they tell

I will imagine their thoughts,
Their love for the earth they live on:
I think of a tree poised
Above a pool of flowers....
This is more to me than legend.

Lullaby

Drowsy, drowsy are the stars In the dark blue
sky.
The moon comes like the mother of the world
And kisses them goodnight.
One by one people shut up their day-tired eyes
And sleep...and dream...
Hiding behind the lilac bush
I have heard dreams come.
Drowsy, drowsy are the winds,
Faint with almond petals,
Rosy with the opening almond flowers;
Tangled in almond boughs or plum boughs. . .
Any Spring sweetness
To bring the drowsy dreams....

Palm Trees

Palm trees like old India shine...

I said to myself:
But really they were folded elm-boughs
Written in shadow
On the grass.

White-Capped Lake

Foam comes and goes;
Stones shine on the lake-bottom...
Waves gurgle like bells.
A maple curves over that lake
To see its shadow.
The lake is clear with dew and wind;
The wind blows a little music
To that tree.

All I have heard and seen and thought
Will go away.
The maple tree will be there still,
But the bright water gone.
The tree will bend until I think of the lake, make
it real again.
Make it shine again under green leaves
Of my mind.

The Forgotten River

There was a river in a dream I had
Now it has gone.
Now it lies lost
At the bottom of my heart.
Not till I find the gold at the end of the rainbow
Can it stir and flow and live
As other rivers do.

Waking The Moths

White as pearls would be on a bed of moss,
I awake them one by one
From their sleepy hours
On the under side of meadow-grasses
To their happy hours of flitting.
I shake the grasses...
They scatter softly...
Airy and light and uncertain
I watch them vanishing.

Weeping Willow

Drooping her eyes,
Looking long into the sky-blue lake,
The willow stands on her island.

Tears are falling gently;
You cannot see them...
What could comfort her?

Some day a wind will blow
A western wind...
Out of heaven's bosom
A breeze will come flying with a harp around its
neck...
Into the willow branches it will fly
And the harp will sing a happy tune.
I know how they sing,
Those harps of the wind,
When the wind Is sorry
Or puzzled!

Costume

I had ribbons the color of daffodils
That are bells within bells:
I had shoes with crystal heels
To keep me dancing:
I tossed my head under a cap
With a tassel of cherries,
And then I said and said once more
My name is Miranda.

South Wind

When the south sang like a nightingale
It was the hour bringing the tinted dawn.
Over the meadow's grassy breast
I trod with trembling feet:
I rested on moss:
My thoughts glittered...
I felt I could touch them.
My hair was blowing...fell around me...
I heard the nightingale wind
Like magic in mist:
It was then I said to the thick trees
"Why try to pretend?
You cannot hide the world from me:
It is looking at me through your fingers."

Pine Tree

Away in the great forest
On the slope of a snow-capped mountain
A lonely pine tree stood by itself.
It had no one to love it:
So I stayed all night
Under its branches laden with snow.
I did not mind the cold.

Clarke Farm

As you wander down a road of golden sand
You look past stretches of winter-dry meadow
Inlaid with spruce and pine.
Red maples splash down the forest hillside;
Transparent birches draw pale lines against the
underbrush;
The Connecticut has just now gone swinging be-
tween those mountains, Though I could not see it
going.
The mountains curve downward, they hold their
hands over their eyes...
They peer into the water curiously
Over the tops of yellow willows.
I am far away ... I see the mountains
blurred...Bent heads...blue shoulders...

Crystal Cave

(Bermuda)

The sea is quiet
Within the cave...
The sea hangs from a topaz thread
In a silver bowl.

The trembling sea
Hangs and glitters
And is gone.

April With Veiled Arms

April with veiled arms
And body like a swan's wing,
Opal and bronze in your hair,
Gold in your eyes,
Are you a woman
Out of the sea?
Did you come last night
From the uncurled wave?

Peace-of-Our-Own

Sitting alone in the peace-time
When day turns shadowy
My mother and I read...wonder...
Make poems about beautiful things
We have known and seen.
I have names for many songs
I have not yet made...
Iris...Sun-rays...
Sun-down...or the Moon-Dark...

Or that queer blue song about a peacock feather.
I never know why it is
But whenever I listen
In flies a poem.

Lonely Song

Bend low, blue sky,
Touch my forehead;
You look cool...bend down...
Flow about me in your blueness and coolness.
Be thistledown, be flowers,
Be ail the songs I have not yet sung.
Laugh at me, sky!
Put a cap of cloud on my head,
Blow it off with your blue winds...
Give me a feeling of your laughter
Beyond cloud and wind!
I need to have you laugh at me
As though you liked me a little.

I Thought

I thought the sea was honeycomb
And all the waves were bees
Humming cozily among the foam.

I thought that white mulberry trees
Shook their blossoms out all day
In foam of honey, windy spray:
And then I made a song of these
After I got home.

Cliffacre

A rambling house on top of a cliff
Overlooking a many-colored canyon
Alone with the sunset,
Alone with the dawn.
Trees crowding down beyond the garden:
A place where I should put food for wild ani-
mals...
Through my big west windows
I could watch them come and go.
Sand along the cliff...cedars with berries like blue
wax...
Then the stable half-hidden where I shall keep
my horses
Barberry and Gray Glory,
Just a tile-roofed shelter for them in a wing of
sand
Off at one side...but not too far...

Where will it be? I think ... in Wyoming.
A cliff somewhere ... I know I can find it...
An acre of land for my house and garden.
I shall have a wild silver fox for a pet;
He will learn my ways.
Doors will stand always open...
I shall do as I please all day in that house.
There will be bowls
For short-stemmed flowers;
(I want all flowers that like that country
To live in my garden...)
There will be twenty-four vases
To keep tilled with roses.

Jeanne D'arc

If I were Jeanne D'Arc
It would be hard remembering the apple-orchard
in bloom,
With nothing about me but noise and armies,
All men, all women, unhappy.
No time for children (Let them be quiet!)
No time for anybody
But kings...
And the appletrees all the time wondering ..

Wild Canary

Like a lump of fresh gold
You shine
On an old dead tree you sit
As though you were not a bird at all
But trying your best to seem real,
To give me a thought of wings.

Books

Books, books that I love so,
Poetry...fairy-tales...stories...
All of them together make one huge book
Broad as a mountain
With golden pages
And pictures of long ago.
I read and I read ... of living ... of thoughts...
Of queer things people tell:
If I could I would buy that huge book,
All the world in one!
But it cannot be bought
For one penny or two.

I Was Thinking

I was thinking
The tenderness children need
Is in soft shadow-things;
Is a kind of magic...
Petals of a dark pansy...
Cloudy wings....
(But the sun can touch me
With fingertips like flowers...)

And the tenderness children need
Is in old thoughts and songs of all the world
People have not forgotten...

It is in the way mothers look at tired children.
It is in the half-voice fathers use
Feeling some surprise and gladness
To see their children there at all.

Big Dipper

The Big Dipper spilled stars down over the roofs,
I felt the way the wind whirled stars
Over the town roofs....

I felt the town asleep:
I felt people there in the great crisp dark.
When morning came in a waver of light
There was a breath of change ... all the dreams
going away from the dreamers
As dreams do go away in the morning.

A ring of hills...one river...some streets
Make a design.
Stars make a design
And it is a Big Dipper
Or the Pleiades like a bunch of grapes....
It is harder to say what the roofs mean:
I don't know...
Maybe I'm not yet far enough
Away.

Never-Known

The chickadee taught me this river
Through the goldenrod field;
A river of blue light
Going zigzag over the goldenrod
In the sun.

I found a mountain...

At least it was one to the ants and crickets:
It was round soft turf,
It had a dimple where a stone had been
And a stalk of goldenrod
Instead of an elm tree.

Once I saw a field full of gentians
The color of mountains when they are far away.
But this was an ordinary field
Where a mouse could live quietly all his days
Exploring his own country.
Only to me it was different...
To me it was a Never-Known
With a blue river and a yellow jungle...
And while I was about it, I made my mountains high,
Feathery on top, as they do in maps.
Curved feathers dropped along in handfuls
Marked *Mts.*

This Day

I never asked the day to be good to me
Yet it has been sweet in its going.

This day began behind the moon

Where all the white things come from.
Thistledown comes from behind the moon,
And that clearness of early hours....
But the clearness of this day turned into color
When the sun came.

Now it is dark: now it is bedtime.
I can see the color as though it had not gone,
I can see it better than when it was here:
Even the moon of those early hours of morning
Is more like mother-of-pearl
Or pink silver.

Mother-of-pearl Moon,
Your lonely face grows warm...
You have changed all of a sudden...
You make me think of flowers.

Deserted House

Do you remember the house
With many windows?
It looked through its cobwebs
At the blue mountain.
There were old rosebushes near the doorstep...
Queer bright single roses bloomed...

I used to think of people
Who had wanted them there.
Maybe there was a little girl
Going barefoot...
Maybe she thought summer began
With a rosebush.
Do you remember the maples
And the fence where we saw baby swallows
In a row ?

I made a song about a princess.
She was a little girl...

In the cobweb house of stone she is hidden...
They have left her alone.

Deserted House

When she called no one answered...
They have left her alone.
She sang to keep her heart high...
They have left her alone.
But the silvery cold made her shiver and sleep
And her song went by.

After that I made a story about her

Out of the old house:
I put roseleaves on her eyes...
(You know how sunset. . . every afternoon...
Used to fill the window-panes with colors
They had never known?)

Dragon Fly

You jerk against the sun,
You twist your diamond wires and green-gold
scales,
You tilt your body...head down...
You quiver...
Are you angry or only excited?
I should think the ferns might be excited
Feeling you there:
And you never mention the reasons
For your coming
Sure of your wings
You have time in the air for thinking:
You poise and are content.
But only lizards among old stones
Can find as you find the unexpected turning:
You say *It is time to go!*
And you have gone.

I Shall Come Back

I shall be coming back to you
From seas, rivers, sunny meadows, glens that
hold secrets:
I shall come back with my hands full
Of light and flowers.
Brooks braided in with sunbeams
Will hang from my fingers.
My heart will be awake...
All my thoughts and joys will go to you.
I shall bring back things I have picked up,
Traveling this road or the other.
Things found by the sea or in the pine-wood.
There will be a pine-cone in my pocket,
Grains of pink sand between my fingers.
I shall tell you of a golden pheasant's feather;
I shall tell you of stars like seaweed.
Moons will glitter in my hair...
Will you know me ?
I shall come back when sunset has turned away
and gone,
And you will untangle the moons
And make me drowsy
And put me to bed.

Time

Time is a harp
That plays to you till you fall asleep;
You are always spending it away
Like a music...
Suddenly you are left alone
On a trail of wind.

The mountains were asleep
Long ago!
Listen...the tune is changing...
Do you hear it?
You will sleep too
Before long...

Made in the
USA
Monee, IL